ESCAPE AND EVASION

SPECIAL FORCES: PROTECTING, BUILDING, TEACHING, AND FIGHTING

AIR FORCE

ARMY RANGERS

ELITE FORCES SELECTION

ESCAPE AND EVASION

GREEN BERETS

MARINES

NAVY SEALS

URBAN WARFARE

PARACHUTE REGIMENT

WORLD'S BEST SOLDIERS

ESCAPE AND EVASION

by Jack Montana

Mason Crest Publishers

MASON CREST PUBLISHERS INC.
370 Reed Road
Broomall, Pennsylvania 19008
(866)MCP-BOOK (toll free)
www.masoncrest.com

First Printing
9 8 7 6 5 4 3 2 1

Library of Congress Cataloging-in-Publication Data
Montana, Jack.
  Escape and evasion / by Jack Montana.
    p. cm. — (Special forces : protecting, building, teaching and fighting)
  Includes bibliographical references and index.
  ISBN 978-1-4222-1840-2   ISBN (series) 978-1-4222-1836-5
  1. Special forces (Military science)—United States—Juvenile literature. 2. Infiltration (Military science)—Juvenile literature. 3. Combat survival—Juvenile literature. 4. Survival skills—Juvenile literature. I. Title.
  UA34.S64M384 2011
  335.4—dc22
                          2010020680

Produced by Harding House Publishing Service, Inc.
www.hardinghousepages.com
Interior design by MK Bassett-Harvey.
Cover design by Torque Advertising + Design.
Printed in USA by Bang Printing.

With thanks and appreciation to the U.S. Military for the use of information, text, and images.

Contents

Introduction

Elite forces are the tip of Freedom's spear. These small, special units are universally the first to engage, whether on reconnaissance missions into denied territory for larger conventional forces or in direct action, surgical operations, preemptive strikes, retaliatory action, and hostage rescues. They lead the way in today's war on terrorism, the war on drugs, the war on transnational unrest, and in humanitarian operations as well as nation building. When large-scale warfare erupts, they offer theater commanders a wide variety of unique, unconventional options.

Most such units are regionally oriented, acclimated to the culture and conversant in the languages of the areas where they operate. Since they deploy to those areas regularly, often for combined training exercises with indigenous forces, these elite units also serve as peacetime "global scouts," and "diplomacy multipliers," beacons of hope for the democratic aspirations of oppressed peoples all over the globe.

Elite forces are truly "quiet professionals": their actions speak louder than words. They are self-motivated, self-confidant, versatile, seasoned, mature individuals who rely on teamwork more than daring-do. Unfortunately, theirs is dangerous work. Since the 1980 attempt to rescue hostages from the U.S. embassy in Tehran, American special operations forces have suffered casualties in real-world operations at close to fifteen times the rate of U.S. conventional forces. By the very nature of the challenges that face special operations forces, training for these elite units has proven even more hazardous.

Thus it's with special pride that I join you in saluting the brave men who volunteer to serve in and support these magnificent units and who face such difficult challenges ahead.

—Colonel John T. Carney, Jr., USAF–Ret.
President, Special Operations Warrior Foundation

CHAPTER 1

What It Takes to Work Behind Enemy Lines

Special Forces units go behind enemy lines to gather intelligence, rescue prisoners, or destroy enemy equipment. Since World War II, Special Forces engaged in many kinds of **unconventional warfare**, sabotaging enemies, or going undercover to fight terrorists and **guerilla** soldiers. Undercover operations require soldiers who can place themselves in a foreign society and blend in. This book reveals the skills and qualities needed to be an undercover warrior in the twenty-first century. Surviving behind enemy lines demands

UNDERSTAND THE FULL MEANING

unconventional warfare: Unlike conventional warfare, unconventional warfare uses secretive methods that support one side of an existing conflict, using techniques such as psychological attacks and sabotage.

guerilla: Referring to a type of warfare that uses surprise raids and sabotage to harass the enemy.

intelligence, creative thinking, and self-control. It's not easy. The men who complete these missions are some of the world's most skilled soldiers.

The U.S. Army has many tests that determine who can survive the stress of being behind enemy lines. They devised a list of seven different characteristics that undercover soldiers must have:

- They must be resistant to mental and physical tiredness.
- They must be able to solve difficult problems.
- They must be team-workers.
- They must face danger with resolution, courage, and intelligence.
- They must have the ability to remember military information.
- They must show willingness to work hard in training.
- They must have the ability to survive isolation and work on their own.

If a recruit shows these qualities, he can qualify to be an undercover elite soldier.

An amazing variety of combat, survival, and tactical skills are required to complete missions. These include:

- Using weapons, including rifles, machine guns, explosives, and other methods of destroying tanks and aircraft.

- The ability to navigate across difficult terrain and not get lost.
- Tracking the enemy over long distances while hidden.
- Communicating with others using new forms of technology.
- Precisely directing artillery fire and air strikes at their targets.
- Setting and detecting mines and booby traps.
- Surviving in mountains.
- Using first-aid skills.
- Sailing and diving.

Surviving in Special Forces Missions

Performing special combat operations requires a resilient mind. You need a large amount of mental concentration to make crucial decisions and look ahead while surviving to complete a mission. In the two American wars of the twenty-first century (Iraq and Afghanistan), war has been less conventional than in previous twentieth-century conflicts. Because of this, special missions in the military have become increasingly stressful. Many have compared stress levels in today's wars to a faucet that goes from cold to hot in an instant.

Training in the Special Forces may be hard, but being in the field and actually completing difficult missions is even harder. You need nerves of steel to perform these missions.

Training specialized forces like the U.S. Navy SEALs can take years and large amounts of money.

Undercover soldiers do not only perform in combat situations. Special forces soldiers may go into a foreign village

SEAL training is time-consuming, expensive and difficult—these Basic Underwater Demolition/SEAL (BUDs) students are participating in Surf Passage, one of many physically demanding evolutions that are a part of the first phase of SEAL training.

and befriend the locals. By doing this, the soldier is able to gather intelligence on the enemy or build trust so that later on civilians can assist in fighting the enemy. For instance, the U.S. Fifth Special Forces Group (5SPG) in the Vietnam War trained the Civilian Irregular Defense Groups, bands

Observation Skills

Observation is one of the most important skills for undercover soldiers, who must be alert at all times. This means that they use all their senses to take in as much information from the world around them. Nothing must be missed. The soldier must be aware of colors, shapes, movements, noises, odors, and sensations. Anything could provide a vital clue about danger approaching. In the Vietnam War, for example, trampled grass, signs of garbage, or even a single twig out of place by the side of a road might have indicated to a U.S. patrol that there was a booby trap or ambush waiting for them. By reading these warnings, troops can stay one step ahead of the enemy.

of Vietnamese civilians who fought on their side against the communists. Special Forces units in Vietnam enlisted 42,000 civilian soldiers by making friends with locals.

It takes more than combat skills to be a successful undercover soldier. Several other skills are also needed. An **elite** soldier should be able to learn a new language and speak

UNDERSTAND THE FULL MEANING

elite: The best and most skilled of a group.

that language fluently—which means he can speak comfortably without stumbling over words or using awkward phrases. He should also have good relational skills; this means being able to negotiate with people. Undercover sol-

Training Iraqis in Combat Techniques

Combat troops need to make sure they have relational skills. Winning over public opinion in an occupied territory can be important. Recently, American Special Forces units have taught the occupied Iraqi army the military techniques and tactics found in this book. In April 2010, a group of American troops taught twenty-two Iraqi Army Special Forces combat techniques. They taught them sniping, stalking, and detecting targets. The also taught skills in camouflage and helped them make their own ghillie suits using burlap bags and camouflage materials.

diers must have the ability to impersonate people if they want to blend with foreign peoples during an operation. By observing the way people dress, speak, act, and think, they are able to imitate these characteristics.

Undercover soldiers must be able to keep a secret. Those that want to be an undercover soldier so they can brag about it are never accepted into the job. The U.S. military trusts soldiers to keep highly secret information. If a soldier boasted about his work to his parents, spouse, or friends, he would put lives in danger. In some cases, undercover soldiers must hold these secrets for the rest of their lives.

Next we will see how enemy soldiers end up behind enemy lines, the skill known as "infiltration," the ability to go behind enemy lines without being noticed.

Using tall grass for cover, a soldier sets up his shot using the "buddy-supported" firing position, taking aim with his M110 Sniper Rifle. The snipers trained Iraqi Army Special Forces soldiers as part of a two-week sniper training course in Mosul, Iraq.

CHAPTER 2
Infiltrating by Air

Most elite units train soldiers in parachute techniques. They need to know how to perform a static line drop, in which a large number of troops jump from an aircraft and parachute down to the ground. This method is usually too slow, and transport aircrafts can easily be shot down—so the military designed new methods of parachuting.

A swifter, more secret way is called High-Altitude, Low-Opening (HALO) parachuting. Troops jump from an aircraft at an altitude of 32,000 feet (10,000 m). They do not open their parachutes immediately but instead, freefall until 2,500 feet (760 m) and then open their parachutes. This means they get from the aircraft to the ground quickly and are less likely to be found by the enemy.

HALO parachuting requires a lot of training. The freefaller has to keep a stable position during the flight while wearing a heavy backpack and weapon strapped to his body. At high altitudes, the HALO jumpers need oxygen-breathing equipment. The fall is so fast that HALO parachuting requires a machine called a "barometric trigger" to automatically open

Landing by Helicopter

When an elite forces unit lands by helicopter, they must follow this procedure:

- Get out of the helicopter as quickly as possible, keeping low to avoid the rotor blades spinning above their heads.

- Adopt defensive positions immediately on all sides of the helicopter, since the noise of the helicopter will mean that they cannot hear gunfire if the enemy is shooting at them.

- Spend two or three minutes after the helicopter has left getting used to the silence and environment. This means sitting still without talking, listening and watching carefully for signs of an approaching enemy.

- Work out exactly where the helicopter has dropped the unit before moving off.

parachutes at the right altitude. The difficulties don't stop there; paratroopers are exposed to freezing temperatures as they freefall. This can result in ice forming on their equipment, especially their goggles. HALO jumpers need to be in prime shape and highly skilled. The U.S. military spends a large amount of time training for HALO jumps, but only the best elite units train their soldiers in HALO techniques.

There are other techniques that are used to transport soldiers safely behind enemy borders. HAHO parachuting stands for High-Altitude, High-Opening parachuting. HAHO paratroopers drop from an aircraft wearing oxygen-breathing equipment at an altitude of 32,000 feet (10,000 m). They freefall for only 8 to 10 seconds and then open the parachute around 27,600 feet (8,500 m). They then slowly and silently float to the ground. This can take between 70 to 80 minutes and they travel for up to 19 miles (30 km). This means that the team can drop outside enemy territory and drift behind enemy lines unseen by radar. There are problems with HAHO parachuting. The special forces team must stay together once parachutes are opened to land in the same location. Winds can scatter people for miles, so this is difficult. Soldiers must be experts at using parachutes so they can land close together.

Elite teams can also simply land an aircraft on a runway and unload Special Forces units. Aircraft such as the Lysander require an airstrip of at least 300 feet (92 m); heavier transports need a runway of at least 1,200 feet (370 m) to land and take off safely. If an established runway isn't available, a rough strip will have to be built. Elite teams arrive and leave during darkness, so the airstrip will need some illumination to guide in the pilot.

Once on the ground, the leader gathers the team. Each member will have memorized their meeting location, called

A jumpmaster checks a soldier's parachute during a training exercise at Fort Bragg, N.C.

the rendezvous point. To assist in gathering the team, the commander will activate a portable radio homing beacon that emits a high-frequency signal. When the other team members land, they activate their personal handheld radio receivers, which pick up signals and convert the signals into

Jumpmaster

"Jumpmaster" is a respected military title used for a specialist in airborne deployment and combat. He supervises other paratroopers jumping from a plane. Training is a nearly month-long process, and not everyone makes it. For instance, when training in October of 2009, 37 out of 51 trainees became jumpmasters when training at Fort Carson, Colorado. The title of jumpmaster is looked at highly because of the great responsibility that goes along with the position.

Colorado training officer Patrick Clark states the importance of being a jumpmaster: "This is a job that we take seriously because every jumpmaster is responsible for every parachutist and the number-one rule is never sacrifice safety for any reason." Attention to detail is especially important because "a lack of attention to detail can result in lost lives. From the time the jumpmaster receives the order until the time everyone is on the ground, the jumpmaster is responsible."

a bleeping noise. The signal becomes stronger when they get closer. Once gathered at the rendezvous point, the team buries their parachute equipment. No trace of their landing is left.

Helicopters are the most popular method of infiltration. The United States leads the way with helicopter technology. Helicopters such as the UH-60 Black Hawk can fly at treetop level, which is underneath enemy radars. It is dangerous to fly at this altitude, and helicopters fly at a speed of 90 miles per hour (140 km/h). At these speeds, pilots are able to fly

These soldiers are simulating a freefall in a mud pit during pararescue training.

Freefall Training

In training, free fallers learn a lot in a short amount of time. They must be able to parachute down to safety in highly hazardous environments. Often, they must do this in stealth or at night. The terrain and weather conditions may also change the situations into which military units infiltrate behind military lines. There is a lot to learn during training.

During a four-week course in Fort Bragg, North Carolina, students fly through wind tunnels, as well as learn new techniques such as mass exits, grouping exercises, night operations, and using oxygen gear. At the same time, they are learning to use combat equipment.

helicopters using night-vision goggles, which allow them to see in the dark. Flying at these altitudes means being vulnerable to enemy ground fire.

Once the helicopter arrives at their destination—called a "Drop Zone"—the team must get out as quickly as possible. They throw their packs out of the helicopter doors and jump out with their guns. These soldiers are prepared for action the moment they hit the ground.

Infiltrating enemy lines by air has many advantages; it is quick and stealthy. However, sometimes other methods are needed.

CHAPTER 3

Infiltrating by Water and Land

nfiltration across sea or land requires precise concentration and tough nerves. Military units must be nearly silent the whole time.

WATER INFILTRATION

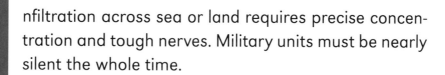

Rivers and coastlines offer elite force units another way of getting into enemy territory undetected. Waterborne operations require troops who are highly trained in using underwater breathing equipment. Teams using scuba equipment infiltrate harbors and rivers, and either move farther inland or carry out sabotage missions against shipping or coastal targets. Elite units such as U.S. Navy SEALS use oxygen tanks that do not let out clouds of bubbles when the soldier breathes out. (If they did, an enemy soldier on a ship might see the bubbles and know there was a diver below.) Special tanks give the soldier four hours of underwater breathing. Each diver must carry his equipment and explosives. **Limpet** mines are stuck on sides of ships and can weigh up to 33 pounds (17 kg). Because of the exertion involved in military diving, the maximum distance for a combat swim is around nine-tenths of a mile (1.5 km).

Because of the problem of swimming to the target, elite units use special floating vehicles to take teams to the target. The subskimmer is a semi-inflatable "boat" that can travel on the surface of the sea and can go underwater. To turn it into a submarine, soldiers seal off the engine and instrument compartment, and then deflate the side tubes. The subskimmer can approach the target underwater, powered by two electric motors. The crew can leave it parked on the seabed while they carry out their mission.

SEALS use the Mark 8 Swimmer Delivery Vehicle (SDV), which can carry six soldiers. It is 30 feet (9 m) long and three feet (90 cm) wide, and shaped like a torpedo. Powered by electric motors, the SDV can maintain an underwater speed of three to four **knots** (5.5–7.5 km) for several hours. The soldiers sit astride the SDV in their wet suits and their breathing equipment in a crouched posture that is

UNDERSTAND THE FULL MEANING

limpet: Usually refers to a shellfish that clings to rocks, but can also mean an explosive device that is designed to cling to something underwater such as the hull of a ship.

knots: A unit of speed. One knot is equal to one nautical mile per hour, or 1.15 mph (1.85 kmph).

A Navy diver stands by to assist a special operator, both from a SEAL Delivery Team (SDV), with SDV operations with the nuclear-powered submarine USS Florida. The diver is training for material certification, which will allow him to perform real-world operations anytime, anywhere.

physically tiring. This means they have to rest onshore for several hours after their journey to recuperate.

Boats and **dinghies** offer a faster way of getting elite forces onto a shore or riverbank, but there are dangers involved with small boats. They have little protection and, if spotted, can be blown out of the water with relative ease. Outboard motors are noisy, but if the team decides to use oars or paddles, it takes longer to get to their destination. Small boats do have several advantages: they can transport large quantities of weapons and equipment, while providing access to areas that are **impenetrable** to foot patrols, such as dense jungles.

LAND INFILTRATION

To infiltrate during land missions, the military uses different vehicles. Land rovers and a range of trucks can transport teams. Land Rovers carry a combination of machine guns, grenade launchers, anti-tank missiles, and Stinger surface-to-air missiles. High Mobility Multi-Purpose Wheeled Vehicles (HMMWV) are designed to operate on all types of terrain

UNDERSTAND THE FULL MEANING

dinghies: Small open boats.

impenetrable: Unable to be entered.

image intensifiers: Devices that allow people to see in low light, such as night-vision glasses.

thermal imagers: Devices that show the heat given off by people and objects, allowing them to be seen in darkness or through walls.

and during any kind of weather. Elite teams favor nighttime hours for travel by land in vehicles since this reduces the chance of convoys being spotted, especially by air.

Human Torpedoes

During World War II, British commandos used what were known as "human torpedoes" to sneak into German harbors and destroy and damage ships. These were boats that were shaped like torpedoes, but had seating on them for commando divers. The commandos would steer these boats under the hulls of German ships. Then the front of the boat, which contained explosives, was detached and left under the German boat to explode when the commandos were at a safe distance.

But vehicles are not the only way elite teams can infiltrate enemy territory. They can also simply walk across borders, although highly defended borders offer major obstacles. Modern borders can be guarded by many sophisticated defenses such as night-vision cameras and invisible microwave beams, which trigger alarms. Watchtowers manned by guards, as well as barbed wired and ditches filled with anti-personnel mines are possible dangers Special Forces may encounter. At times, darkness offers little cover, since the enemy can employ **image intensifiers** and **thermal imagers**, which allow them to see the troops moving during even the darkest night. Because of these defenses, elite forces teams prefer air or waterborne infiltration over travelling by land.

CHAPTER 4
Night Operations

The night is a friend of Special Forces units. It lets teams infiltrate and move through and across enemy lines unseen. It provides cover for rapid withdrawal. But operating in darkness requires special training and preparation. Night fighting puts unique strains on the human body.

The first problem that must be overcome at night is simply that the soldiers cannot see as well as in daylight. Human beings have a certain amount of night vision because we have special cells in our eyes called rods. These rods need at least 30 minutes to get used to darkness and start to work properly. In addition, harsh sunlight makes seeing at night difficult for another 36 hours. Because of this, elite troops wear sunglasses during the day if they will operate at night.

At night, the eyes also have problems estimating distance. Small objects seem farther away, and large objects seem closer. Hearing becomes more acute at night because of a lower level of background noise, and cold, moist air carries sound better. Soldiers can be trained to listen for certain sounds (for example, a rifle bolt being loaded can be heard from a great distance if you know what it sounds like).

The sense of smell can be used at night also. Elite troops train to face at an angle into the wind, and then to relax and breathe normally while taking sharp, frequent sniffs. This way, the soldier can pick up different smells, which may give clues as to the presence of an enemy.

Tired soldiers are a problem during night operations. Elite teams need to make allowance for the fatigue they may experience when operating at night. Every member should be allowed to get some rest, including frequent breaks for food and water. A tired soldier cannot operate at full potential.

Silent movement at night is essential for Special Forces missions. Training emphasizes moving slowly with small, high steps, feeling carefully before shifting the weight onto the leading foot, while at the same time scanning ahead. Troops moving in single file must try to step in the footsteps of the soldier in front of them, since those spaces will have been cleared of obstacles. This tactic will not only help silent

WHY DOES SOUND MOVE FASTER IN COLD AIR?

Sound waves move faster through dense material—and cold air is denser than warm.

Airmen from the U.S. Air Force Special Tactics Training Squadron jump at night on a high altitude, low opening or HALO, training mission.

movement; it will also deceive the enemy as to the size of the unit. Branches and brushes should be pushed aside carefully when moving and then replaced. If they are broken, they will leave white spots on the sides of trees or shrubs, which are highly visible at night.

When moving at night, soldiers lift each leg slowly to nearly knee height. Beginning with the left leg, the soldier balances on the right foot and then eases forward, while

Seeing in Darkness

Scientists and researchers working for the military have been trying to find more efficient ways to help Special Forces units see in the dark. Sergeant Milinda Williams of the U.S. Army Research, Development and Engineering Command states, "At night it can be dark, but nothing is ever completely dark . . . you always have some form of light whether it is the stars, the moon or some small artificial light." The army has been researching night vision for decades. Researchers are currently working on integrating night vision devices on weapons, surveillance, and vehicles. Milinda Williams continues, "It's great, but we continue to work on making battlefield conditions better and brighter." In the future, we can expect to see more advances in night vision technology.

at the same time feeling for dangers such as trip wires or twigs. The toe of the left foot is pointed down and used to feel the ground with the outside of the toe of the boot. If all is clear, the toe is settled on the ground, then the heel, all the time feeling for loose rocks. When he is confident he is on solid footing, the soldier rolls his weight forward and then, following a slight pause, begins to lift his right boot.

Another tactic used at night when moving is called stalking or "the stalk." The stalk is a way of slowly walking at night in a crouch. Often, stalking is done by crawling, because a crawling soldier is difficult for the enemy to see. The fastest crawl is made by pressing the arm and foot on the same side of the body against the ground to pull or push forward. This method can be rather noisy; a quieter way involves pressing down an arm and a foot on opposite sides and resting on one hip. An even quieter method of crawling involves using toes and elbows to lift and move the torso forward slowly. When crawling, the soldier feels for twigs and rocks, and either removes them or goes around them.

Night fighting requires a great deal of training and practice. Precisely identifying targets at night may be difficult. Night fighting teams may put reflective or **luminous** marks on trees or rocks to tell the soldiers where their comrades are. The height of the spots will be known to each member of the team, which helps for aiming. Members of the team will memorize the area in front of them so they can picture it at night. Luminous dots help them keep track of where features are. If an enemy approach is heard, special force soldiers can fire directly at targets, even without seeing them. If footsteps are heard in dry bushes, for example, a soldier

UNDERSTAND THE FULL MEANING

luminous: Giving off light.

will be able to picture the area and know where the sounds are coming from in relation to his position.

When it comes to night fighting on the battlefield, some weapons are more effective than others. Rifles and machine guns enable shooters to spot their targets when night vision devices are used. Image-intensifying sights are an excellent way of seeing in the dark. These sights operate by showing low levels of visible light 100,000 times brighter to let

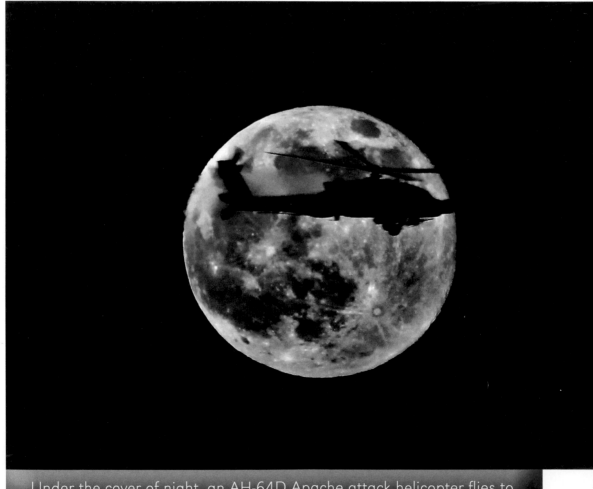

Under the cover of night, an AH-64D Apache attack helicopter flies to conduct operations in Iraq.

soldiers see in the darkest of nights. Because they are light-weight, image intensifiers are often mounted on rifles and machine guns, or soldiers can carry them by hand. They are undetectable by an adversary. Image intensifiers are not as effective in smoke, dense foliage, fog, and heavy rain or snow. The thermal imager (TI) operates like a television camera but creates a picture using infrared "heat" differences instead of light. A TI system operates through smoke, foliage, or camouflage, by day or by night.

By using technology and stealth, the elite soldier can fight and move at night with all the confidence he would have in daylight.

Seeing at Night

When looking at an object in darkness, elite soldiers train themselves to look at the edge of the object rather than straight at it. This is because the human eye sees better at an angle in conditions of darkness. Try this experiment: In a dark room, look at a closed door with a light behind it. If you stare into the center of the door, its outline will start to disappear. If you look at its outline, you can still make out its shape. The elite forces apply this technique when looking at enemy soldiers at night.

CHAPTER 5
Ambushes

The ambush is without doubt one of the most effective weapons in the Special Forces **armory** when behind enemy lines. However, ambushes need expert planning if they are to work at their best.

An ambush is a surprise attack on an enemy formation with the intention of destroying it. The key to an ambush is shock action—a quick attack followed by a speedy withdrawal. The action should be over within two minutes, although elite units often finish the job in less than 30 seconds.

An elite ambushing unit is made up of three parts: the support element, the assault element, and the security element. The support element is usually made up of the commander, radio operators, and medics. The assault element has the task of destroying the enemy in the actual ambush. The security element does just that: provides security. It watches out for any enemy reinforcements and also helps comrades to escape after the attack. In many ways, the security element is one of the most important parts of the operation. Security around the ambush site itself must be tight at all times until the moment when the ambush is sprung.

When planning for an ambush, troops need a lot of information about the enemy. Planning involves working out what type of ambush is required for the task. For example,

Ambush in Afghanistan

Special Forces units were used in Operation Anaconda, the first large battle in Afghanistan since the invasion. Sergeant John Chapman took part in a raid to insert a special operations team on top of a group of Taliban insurgents. They were deployed by helicopter, which crashed under enemy gunfire. He called air-force support to cover their team while they searched for a Navy SEAL who had fallen out of the helicopter.

They came upon an ambush and the enemies fired from all three sides. They attempted a counter-strike to the ambush. Sgt. Chapman broke cover and was killed during the attack, but his actions allowed the unit to survive the ambush.

an ambush against enemy tanks needs antitank weapons and explosives. Timing is one of the most important aspects of the ambush. An ambush sprung in darkness, for example, will achieve more surprise and confusion than one sprung in daylight. The ambushers need to study the ambush site, being careful not to give the enemy any clues that an

Using a terrain model allows soldiers to more effectively plan for operations by recreating the physical characteristic of an area in a miniature version. The model also gives planners the ability to predict possible enemy ambushes based on terrain layout.

ambush is going to take place. In addition to this, the elite forces commander will find out all about the enemy that is to be ambushed, including the number of soldiers, their weapons, and where they will be. Once he has this information, the ambush commander will select the ambush site

Sgt. Leigh Ann Hester, vehicle commander, 617th Military Police Company, Richmond, Ky., stands at parade rest after receiving the Silver Star.

Courage Under Fire

Sgt. Leigh Ann Hester of the Kentucky National Guard received the Silver Star. She is the first woman since World War II to receive the award for combat action. While serving as a team leader with the 617th Military Police Company at Camp Liberty, Iraq, she was one of three vehicles escorting a group of thirty trucks carrying supplies. Approximately thirty enemy fighters ambushed the group. The enemy fighters had AK-47 assault rifles, machine guns, and rocket-propelled grenades. Sgt. Hester's team was outnumbered five to one. Once attacked, a member of their team, medical specialist Jason Mike, fired at their enemies with both an assault rifle and a light machine gun.

Under heavy gunfire, Hester led her soldiers on a counterattack. They flanked the ambusher's position and cleared trenches they occupied with grenade fire. They cut off their enemies' escape route. Suddenly, the attackers were being attacked. The battle lasted for twenty-five minutes. The insurgents suffered twenty-seven casualties, six were wounded, and the United States forces captured one enemy combatant.

Sgt. Hester's performance shows the mental strength needed to combat an ambush. When you are out-gunned and outnumbered, you can still fight back to outwit the enemy.

itself and put the soldiers in place, ready and waiting. When the enemy arrives, the soldiers can spring the ambush and open fire.

One very important quality elite soldiers need is patience. Once an ambush is set, the soldiers might have to wait for many days until their target arrives. Soldiers who get fidgety and bored will let their attention wander, and they might miss signs that the enemy is approaching them. The majority of Special Forces' work involves watching and waiting for the action to start. That is why elite regiments test a candidate's ability to wait around without complaining.

Once an ambush is over, the commander needs to get the troops out quickly. The noise made by the ambush may have alerted other enemy forces, or reinforcements may already

Spotting an Ambush

The following signs can tell an elite unit that there is an ambush waiting for them:

- Birds fly suddenly out of the trees as if startled.

- Plants growing by the side of the road or track have been disturbed.

- Human footprints can be seen on the ground around them.

- Metal can be seen glinting in the foliage.

- Buildings appear deserted; they may have been cleared out for use in the ambush.

be on their way. The commander will evacuate the ambush site quickly. This is done in stages, with the assault element pulling out first and the security element covering. When pulling out, the idea is to create a maximum deception as the various elements withdraw to their rallying points. If the enemy pursues, the security element will use fire and movement to slow them down. In the case of a pursuit, the various elements of the ambush party may split into small groups to evade the pursuers.

Elite units operating behind enemy lines must also know what to do if they themselves are ambushed. The key to a successful counter ambush is hitting back immediately. Firing right back gives the ambushed team time to escape and confuses the enemy. This helps to boost the unit's morale: a unit that survives an ambush and mounts a successful counterattack is going to feel better about itself, and the enemy will feel worse. At the least, counter-ambush tactics give time for reinforcements to arrive.

The most important element of a counter ambush is to keep moving when firing, either charging the ambushers or running around them and then mounting a counterattack from the flanks. All available firepower should be brought to bear on the ambushers, including automatic fire, explosives, grenades, and even antitank rockets when available.

Care must be taken not to fall into a trap. The ambushers might have set up two ambushes: one for an initial attack and another to attack the counterattack! Elite force units, however, usually see any traps before they actually happen. This is because they are experts in tracking enemy movements and spotting hidden enemy soldiers.

CHAPTER 6
Tracking and Moving

An elite soldier must always know where he is at all times behind enemy lines. If soldiers get lost, then they are more likely to be discovered, and their mission is more likely to fail.

An important aspect of navigation is called "terrain analysis." This means looking at the ground in front of you, then looking at the map, and seeing if there are any differences between the two. Terrain analysis involves things like working out which way the rivers run, which features can be seen at night, and the position of fences and other man-made features. In terrain such as dense jungle, where the only thing to be seen is trees, elite soldiers will have to use their compasses to navigate, which will mean literally holding them in front of them while they walk. At night, the military compasses are luminous so they can still be seen.

Another method of navigating is called "dead reckoning." Dead reckoning means that soldiers plot their journey before they set out on a mission, and plan it in a series of stages. Each one is measured in terms of distance and direction between two points. These courses lead them from the starting point to the final destination. They help the soldiers find out where they are at any one time, either by following

Map Skills

Learning map skills is important in today's missions. Although many computers are used to find coordinates, the ability to find an item on the map cannot be replaced. Adam Zach, a member of a three-person mortar team in Afghanistan, said, "You've got to be good at math and map reading. You also have got to know how to plot points." Zach stated that they do have a light handheld computer into which they put coordinate information, but they still have to be able to read a map manually if the technology stops working.

In today's world of MapQuest and GPSs, only 43 percent of all people surveyed thought that map reading skills were "absolutely necessary." If you are interested in joining the military, however, learning basic map-making can give you an edge.

their plan or comparing where they are on the ground to where they are on the map.

Once they have worked out where they are going and plotted their route on a map, elite soldiers will mark out route

UNDERSTAND THE FULL MEANING

deviate: To turn aside.

cards. These describe each stage of the route they intend to travel. When they have completed their route cards, they are ready to move. When moving, they must keep a careful eye on the direction they are heading and the distance they have covered. If they **deviate** from their route, they must make adjustments to the route cards. However, if they are operating in an area where contact with the enemy is likely, they will not write anything down, because this information may be useful to an enemy if they are captured.

Knowing as much as possible about the enemy will help an elite team find out valuable military information.

An Iraqi airman practices reading a map during the land navigation portion of a basic military training course.

This involves knowing where the enemy is and what he is doing, and this must be done by tracking. A careless enemy will leave telltale signs of his presence, which can then be used against him. Moved stones, crumbled stones, or bent grasses are signs that an enemy patrol has been in the area. Stains are another sign. These may include blood, water on stones, and crushed leaves.

Garbage indicates the presence of ill-disciplined soldiers, though booby traps may have been left among the garbage

Dead Reckoning

Linguists are unsure of how this term started. Some think the term stands for "deduced reckoning," which may have originally been shortened as "ded. reckoning," while others think that it means a reasoning of one's position from a stationary object or one that is "dead in the water." Sailors like Christopher Columbus were the first to adopt dead-reckoning techniques.

to kill the unwary. Sounds can also tell the unit where the enemy is. Soldiers can place their ears on the ground or on a stick driven six inches (15 cm) into the ground to listen. It is hard to work out the direction of the noises, but sounds can be heard from a long distance because the ground actually carries noise better than the air. Sounds will also carry farther in light mist, though rain or wind can mask them. Rain may also cause soldiers to miss sounds if they are wearing hoods or caps, so it can be worth having a wet head in order to hear sounds. During a night operation, no one should wear a hat or helmet. Helmets make hollow sounds in the rain, whistle during breezes, and magnify rattles and rustles.

Poor enemy camouflage can also be a signpost to an attacking team. In particular, team members should look for straight lines (rarely found in nature), unusual differences in color or tone, and unnatural vegetation, such as green leaves among dead branches.

Having detected the enemy, a team must work out their distance to them. This can be difficult. Judging distances depends on a soldier's skill and the amounts of water vapor in the air. Clear, desert air, for example, helps a soldier to detect sights at a greater distance, but does not carry sound or odors as well as more **humid** air. Sounds can be a real problem when estimating distances, since they can bounce among buildings and rocky terrain, misleading an individual as to the direction of their source. Sound travels at around 1,000 feet (300 m) per second, so the elite soldier should count the seconds between seeing the flash of weapon fire and hearing its bang. The number of seconds multiplied by three equates to the distance to the weapon in hundreds of meters.

Even if elite soldiers are master shots with their rifles, or experts at blowing up bridges, they must still learn how to become virtually invisible while doing all these things. This is the art of hiding.

UNDERSTAND THE FULL MEANING

humid: Having a high amount of water or water vapor, especially referring to air that is noticeably damp.

Avoiding the Enemy

Elite soldiers who are behind enemy lines cannot do anything useful if they are caught. The three essential techniques of remaining unseen are known as cover, concealment, and camouflage.

Concealment is the art of preventing yourself from being seen. This may involve natural concealment—such as bushes, grass, and shadows—or artificial, with the soldier using materials such as camouflage nets. Successful concealment, both natural and artificial, may depend on the season, weather, and light.

Soldiers use camouflage to mask the color, outline, or texture of themselves and their equipment. Vegetation or other materials that grow in the area provide natural—and the best—camouflage. When looked at closely, man-made substances will always appear to be man-made. The secret of camouflage is to never draw the attention of the enemy or create a reason for the enemy to investigate your position.

Many things can give you away. These include cut branches when you are building a concealed shelter (known as a hide); poorly concealed hide edges; equipment left outside the hide; and, of course, garbage left outside the hide. A soldier needs to remember than the enemy can smell, too: food should be eaten without cooking if possible. Maintaining stealth and being quiet is important. A soldier should walk as quietly as possible. Anything that might rattle should be taped down to keep it quiet. Team members should send messages through hand signals. Because sound carries best at night, noise of any kind should be reduced to zero.

When communicating, do not imitate birdcalls. Unless your enemy is stupid, they will know these signals are not birds chirping. Most birds call in the early morning and evening. They do not call to each other in the middle of the night. Owls hoot, but how many owls do you hear? Are they native to the area? Owls stick to one area their entire lives. If the enemy has been in an area for several weeks without

Michael Murphy

In 2005, Lieutenant Michael Murphy went on a reconnaissance mission inside enemy territory in Afghanistan. He was on a mission to find a high-level enemy militia leader. While in a very rugged area of terrain, he was discovered by Taliban sympathizers. Very soon, between 30 and 40 enemy fighters attacked Murphy's four-man team. All four team members were wounded. Once the primary communicator for the team was wounded beyond being able to communicate, Murphy risked going into open terrain to get help. Lt. Murphy was shot down while saving the life of his countrymen.

hearing an owl, and then hears two owls hooting back and forth, the special unit's cover will be blown. Any noise you make will be assumed a threat.

When camouflaging yourself, make sure that you avoid the "Five S's"—shape, shine, shadow, silhouette, and spacing. Straight lines—a sign of human presence—should be

Pilots from the 909th Air Refueling Squadron apply camouflage during an evasion exercise, after a KC-135 "crash" at Kadena Air Base, Japan.

avoided. Cover rifle barrels with bits of camouflaged material. Anything reflective or bright should be made dull, from the face (camouflaged with greasepaint) to the heels of boots. Anything smooth should be made rough or crinkly. Movement should be within shadows wherever possible, and creating shadows, even on the body, should be avoided.

Hiding for Long Periods

If elite soldiers need to hide silently in one place for a long time, they will do well to obey the following rules:

- Every hour or so, stretch out each leg so that limbs do not go "dead." This means that they will be able to move quickly if they have to escape.

- Be sure to eat and drink to keep their energy levels up, but do not leave any garbage that could tell the enemy they are there.

- Do mental tasks. Otherwise they may become bored and miss important events in front of them.

Keep away from crests and skylines because you will stand in silhouette.

Soldiers have to be prepared to move slowly to their objective. The enemy—for trainee soldiers, that is the instructors—will notice not only human movement, but sudden flights (and the alarm calls) of birds or animals, odd movement of plants and bushes, and so on. Camouflage has to be the right color, and may have to be changed frequently so that the soldier constantly blends into the background. Also, grass and saplings grow up toward the sun, so a patch of strangely flattened vegetation will instantly raise suspicion.

The best hope a soldier has of remaining invisible when moving in grass and woodland is the "ghillie suit," an outfit made up of hundreds of strips of camouflaged cloth. The soldier wearing this suit may look like a scarecrow, but the camouflage is excellent. The suit, which can take up to 50 hours to make, was created by gamekeepers (ghillies) in the Scottish Highlands in the nineteenth century. A ghillie suit is hot and heavy. But surviving on the modern battlefield has never been comfortable.

In cities, various shades of gray seem to make the most effective camouflage, and here the occasional straight line and smooth surface will blend into the man-made background. White suits, usually looser than standard uniform to break up the human profile, are worn against full snow or ice. Where there is ground snow but none on the trees, wearing a woodland camouflage jacket and white pants is best. In the desert, a ghillie suit should not be worn. Desert environments are the most difficult in which to camouflage yourself. Using sand-colored uniforms in the camouflage suit pattern, and whatever local vegetation there is (if any), are the soldier's best hopes.

When on a **reconnaissance** mission, one of the best ways to stay hidden is by building a camouflaged shelter (a hide). What kind of shelter the soldier builds depends on

UNDERSTAND THE FULL MEANING

reconnaissance: A search made for useful information in the field.

MultiCam Camouflage

In 2010, the military began using a new kind of camouflage called "MultiCam" instead of the normal desert camouflage pattern. The military conducted an evaluation of camouflage used in Afghanistan and found that the MultiCam patterns were most effective, especially in woodland areas. Seven hundred and fifty soldiers were used in detailed tests and interviews to determine what official camouflage pattern would best suit the war. Computer technology also was used in determining what the human eye may see.

MultiCam has background colors of brown and light tan blended with green and yellow tones. There are also light pink blotches that are spread around the pattern to make the appearance of the soldier change when she moves from a desert environment to a wooded one. The effectiveness of this camouflage pattern is measured by how the pattern can be used for multiple missions in Afghanistan.

the mission. A soldier may simply build an arrangement of bushes and grasses to hide for a few minutes. A long **surveillance** mission can involve building a complex shelter with a roof and observation holes to view the enemy. The front of such a hide should be made bulletproof, often by heaping up a bank of soil in front of it. The shelter should be big enough to allow the team some movement; this will

UNDERSTAND THE FULL MEANING

surveillance: Close watch or observation.

help them exercise stiff muscles. Perhaps most important, the hide should not be set up in a position that would be obviously used for reconnaissance. The enemy will likely be watching for obvious spots like the tops of hills.

If soldiers follow these techniques, they should be able to operate behind enemy lines without being discovered. It takes nerves of steel to survive surrounded by the enemy, but the world's elite forces are trained to do just that.

Members of the 3rd Combat Communications Group raise a large camouflage net over shelters and equipment during Operation Desert Shield.

FIND OUT MORE ON THE INTERNET

The Combat Tracking Team
www.military.com/forums/0,15240,123098,00.html

Green Beret Training
www.goarmy.com/special_forces/training.jsp

Survival and Self-Reliance Studies Institute: Survival, Escape, and
Evasion
www.ssrsi.org/ods/sere.htm

Survival Training
www.training.sfahq.com/survival_training.htm

The websites listed on this page were active at the time of publication. The publisher is not responsible for websites that have changed their address or discontinued operation since the date of publication. The publisher will review and update the websites upon each reprint.

FURTHER READING

Bohrer, David. *America's Special Forces: SEALs, Green Berets, Rangers, USAF Special Ops, Marine Force Recon*. St. Paul, Minn.: MBI Publishing, 2002.

Department of Defense. *Guerrilla Warfare and Special Forces Operations*. Washington, D.C.: Pentagon Publishing, 2004.

Department of Defense. *Map Reading and Land Navigation and Special Forces Survival Evasion and Recovery.* Washington, D.C.: Pentagon Publishing, 2010.

Department of the Army. *U.S. Army Guerrilla Warfare Handbook*. New York: Skyhorse Publishing, 2009.

Fowler, Will. *The Special Forces Guide to Escape and Evasion.* New York: Thomas Dunne, 2005.

Potter, Joshua, Mark Monday, and Gary Stubblefield. *Ambush! A Professional's Guide to Preparing and Preventing Ambushes.* Boulder, Colo.: Paladin Press, 2010.

Southworth, Samuel and Stephen Tanner. *U.S. Special Forces: A Guide to America's Special Operations Units, The World's Most Elite Fighting Force.* Cambridge, Mass.: DeCapo Press, 2002.

Thompson, Leroy. *Secret Techniques of the Elite Forces: How to Train and Fight Like the Elite and Special Operations Forces of the World*. Barnsley, South Yorkshire, U.K.: Greenhill Books, 2005.

BIBILIOGRAPHY

"Charles Chibitty." American Indians in the US Army, www.army.mil/americanindians/soldiershonored/c_charleschibitty.html (14 May 2010).

Donley, Michael. "Streamers: Symbols for bravery, patriotism." U.S. Air Force 26 Aug 2009, www.af.mil/information/speeches/speech.asp?id=500 (13 May 2010).

Lopez, C. Todd. "Soldiers to get new cammo pattern for wear in Afghanistan." U.S. Army 20 Feb 2010, www.army.mil/-news/2010/02/20/34738-soldiers-to-get-new-cammo-pattern-for-wear-in-afghanistan/ (14 May 2010).

McFadden, Duff E. "Spartans provide Iraqi army with 'combat multiplier.'" U.S. Army 15 April 2010, www.army.mil/-news/2010/04/15/37442-spartans-provide-iraqi-army-with-combat-multiplier/ (13 May 2010).

McNally, David. "NCO finds night vision enlightening." U.S. Army 17 Mar 2010, www.army.mil/-news/2010/03/17/35961-nco-finds-night-vision-enlightening/ (14 May 2010).

Reeves, Donald. "Rome soldier part of 3-man mortar team in Afghanistan." Rome News Tribune 2 May 2010, romenews-tribune.com/view/full_story/7200680/article-Rome-soldier-part-of-3-man-mortar-team-in-Afghanistan?instance=home_news_lead_story#ixzz0n4Qrwd2B (14 May 2010).

Straight Dope Science Advisory Board. "Is 'dead reckoning' short for 'deduced reckoning'?" The Straight Dope 21 Nov. 2002, www.straightdope.com/columns/read/2053/is-dead-reckoning-short-for-deduced-reckoning (13 May 2010).

"United States Medal of Honor: Operation Enduring Freedom." U.S. Army 4 May 2010, www.army.mil/MedalOfHonor/citations30.html (13 May 2010).

INDEX

ABOUT THE AUTHOR

Jack Montana lives in upstate New York with his wife and three dogs. He writes on military survival, health, and wellness. He graduated from Binghamton University.

ABOUT THE CONSULTANT

Colonel John Carney, Jr. is USAF-Retired, President and the CEO of the Special Operations Warrior Foundation.

PICTURE CREDITS

United States Air Force
    Amanda N. Grabiec: pg. 55
    Angelique Perez: pg. 53
    Benjamin Wiseman: pg. 16
    Clay Lancaster: pg. 33
    Jack Sanders: pg. 30
    James M. Bowman: pg. 8
    Quinton Russ: pg. 49
    Susan Parent: pg. 20
    Veronica Pierce: pg. 23

United States Army
    Gregory Gieske: pg. 15

Jeremy D. Crisp: pg. 42
Sgt Jennifer Cohen: pg. 46
Sgt. Jose Lopez: pg. 59
Travis Zielinski: pg. 36

United States Navy
    Andrew McKaskle: pg. 27
    Ernesto Hernandez Fonte: pg. 41
    John Hulle: pg. 38
    Kathryn Whittenberger: pg. 24
    Kyle D. Gahlau: pg. 12

To the best knowledge of the publisher, all images not specifically credited are in the public domain. If any image has been inadvertently uncredited, please notify Harding House Publishing Service, 220 Front Street, Vestal, New York 13850, so that credit can be given in future printings.